MARRIAGE

FOR WENDY
in celebration of our Diamond Wedding
2 AUGUST 1958 - 2018

Also by John Elinger

That Sweet City: Visions of Oxford (with Katherine Shock)
That Mighty Heart: Visions of London (with Katherine Shock)
That Strange Necessity: Visions of Portmeirion (with Peter Honey)

MARRIAGE
A SONNET SEQUENCE

JOHN ELINGER
2018

SIGNAL BOOKS · Oxford

First published in the UK in 2018 by
Signal Books Limited
36 Minster Road
Oxford OX4 1LY
www.signalbooks.co.uk

ISBN 978-1-909930-69-8 Paper

A catalogue record for this book is available from the British Library

Production: Baseline Arts, Oxford
Cover Design: Baseline Arts, Oxford
Printed in India by Imprint Digital Ltd

Foreword

BY SIR PAUL COLERIDGE

SOMEWHAT WITH TONGUE IN CHEEK, I sometimes say, when talking about the work of *Marriage Foundation*, that I bring to its work my own experience over nine (sic) decades. During that time I have seen and experienced both the best and the worst which marriage, from start to finish, can embrace. The nine decades comprise forty-five years in the family justice system at every level and in every type of case, watching on a more or less daily basis the horribly painful death throes of countless marriages. But for the same duration I have myself been married to the same woman by whom I have three (now married) children and six grandchildren. Like so many who have gone the distance, the longer it lasts the more utterly convinced you become that it is the central core of your existence and stability and, from a human point of view, the well spring of your deepest lifetime contentment and an essential pillar of such success as you achieve. And you dread its termination by death or illness of one or other of your partnership. Those of us who share this experience are truly blessed.

Immersing myself in this most ancient and worldwide of domestic and social arrangements (not "institution" please) for my entire adult life has convinced me that it is almost impossible to distil or extract the essential ingredients, the *sine qua nons*, the absolute essentials of a successful (let alone "happy") marriage. There is no template upon which to construct marriage. For relationships cannot be designed or lived by numbers. As every person on the planet is different so the linking of two in marriage is bound also always to create difference(s). However it is possible to see some frequent and common themes or threads which occur very often.

John Elinger's compendium of sonnets is a treasure trove of such threads and themes mined and honed over a lifetime of his marriage as he approaches his 60th wedding anniversary. Observing and contemplating the marital behaviour he has experienced over half a century has enabled him to identify and focus in on the important and the trivial. And sorting out the lists is not as obvious as might be supposed. Each sonnet finds and describes a new ingredient serious or sad, happy or pain-filled. Over and over again I found myself smiling actually or internally, as a bell rang in my consciousness and conscience.

Nowadays hardly a day goes by without some research-based finding or other underlining the central importance of marriage to a stable, secure and balanced society. But science is only one, narrow, colourless way of measuring success. These little poetic gems remind you of the vitally important emotional facets and thus enable you to feel and see what such a marriage means to so many of the individuals involved.

At the launch of *Marriage Foundation* in 2012 I said that the mistake which was so often made by many young unmarried people was their view that perfect marriages just fell from the sky onto the beautiful people in white linen suits and from then on you would ride off into the sunset, blissfully happy. What a misconception that is! The reality is utterly different. Successful marriages are chiselled out of the rock of human stubbornness and over many, many years. They are held together with string and rusty nails. But at the end you have created something unique, incapable of copying, deeply satisfying like nothing else and more or less indestructible. A house built on a rock capable of withstanding every sling and arrow of life's outrageous fortune. This volume illustrates that truth exactly. Read and savour these nuggets of the large rock of life-long married life.

SIR PAUL COLERIDGE
Chairman of Marriage Foundation
Specialist Family lawyer and Family High Court Judge 1971-2014

INTRODUCTION

THIS SEQUENCE OF ONE HUNDRED AND FORTY-FOUR SONNETS was written between 2014 and 2016 in hopeful anticipation of our Diamond Wedding in 2018. They are dedicated to Wendy, my wife and illustrator, and companion for sixty years – or sixty-one, to be precise: we met, and decided to spend our lives together in 1957. We raised six much-loved children, and are blessed with eight grandchildren – and four great-grandchildren (and counting!).

Coincidentally, while I was working on these poems, our family celebrated the marriages of two of our eldest grand-children: as I wrote, I reflected on the (unlikely) idea that they might value the experience and guidance of those who had gone before – a characteristic that is typical of more primitive cultures, but sadly lost from ours... So, the book is intended for them, too – and perhaps for future generations of our own family and, indeed, for others.

They are a labour of love – both a celebration and a study of marriage, our own and those of other people we know, or have met, or read about. The attentive reader will discover that the poems range across a number of topics intimately related to the subject of marriage: friendship, sex, parenthood, family, infidelity, divorce, bereavement – and refer from time to time to other real and literary marriages that I have found interesting and informative. Poetry is serious: poets mean what they say. I do. Please don't read these verses, if you are kind enough to read them at all, as if they were some kind of ingenious caprice. I have written what I think (and feel) is true.

A recurrent metaphor linking marriage and poetry has allowed me to write about the composition of verse and, more specifically, the challenge of the sonnet-form. But the central theme of these poems is the nature of married love as it develops and matures from the outset of the enterprise of a marriage to its fulfilment and termination. Nothing in my life has meant more to me than this relationship, shared with my wife, neither work, nor family, nor learning – neither ideas, nor things, nor (other) people. Our marriage comes first. I hope it may last for at least a few more years, and perhaps serve to enlighten and encourage others who choose to travel along the same path. We wish them well.

JOHN ELINGER (aka Christopher Ball)

SONNETS

I

While nothing is so difficult as life-
long marriage, nothing's half so valuable.
What you accept becomes acceptable;
trust nourishes trustworthiness. A wife
and husband are like warp and weft, or knife
and fork, united in reciprocal
learning of give and take, of yield and pull,
across the patchwork years of peace and strife.

Cherishing one another teaches care;
partners who share learn better how to share.
You have a common purpose: children are
prime elements that make the marriage work.
List things that please you, not those things that irk.
Start slowly, take your time, the end's still far.

2

Weddings are worthless: marriage is what counts –
a marathon which never ends, a race
where friends and family smile and embrace
you both at the start-line, as you announce
your joint and binding pledge to what amounts
to a life sentence of endurance. Face
the future now, hold hands for ever, pace
yourselves. This is a race you can't renounce.

Divorce will never be an option, since
divorce is marriage by another name:
failed marriages are lifelong just the same.
Trust the survivors: how may we convince
you never to regret what you've begun,
since marriages mature in the long run?

3

Marriage persists: whatever else one thinks
it may be for, a marriage is for keeps.
A full-time job is part-time — no-one sleeps
and works together — but the marriage-link's
alive all day, all night. It never sinks
from sight and consciousness. Life leaps or creeps
along, and people change, but marriage keeps
on keeping on, as changeless as the Sphinx.

'In sickness and in health, for richer and
for poorer, and for better or for worse.'
The young ones speak, the old ones understand
those fearful binding words, this lifelong pledge,
which, once dishonoured, turns into a curse,
but honoured makes marriage a privilege.

4

Marriage admits impediments: love is
not love, which can't accept that human love's
imperfect, nor forgive iniquities.
In marriage, pushes never come to shoves.
No married lovers calculate what's owed
to them, nor overlook the debts they owe:
acceptance, trust, forgiveness, care, bestowed
freely, without demanding *quid pro quo*.
Marital love's not limited by time,
though wedding cakes may stale, and flowers fade.
Marriage improves, and still maintains its prime,
like solemn music some old master made.
    Marriage matures like cheese or vintage wine,
    or verse perfected by that final line.

5

Bright white is wedding colour: bride and cake
wear white and dazzle on that special day –
but not for long, since nothing white can stay.
Cakes crumble into brown crumbs. Brides awake
as wives from dreams of fairyland, forsake
that magic gown for daily life. Away
they go in their 'going-away' dress – grey
or blue – to lives discoloured and opaque.

Marriage turns silver, then to gold at last:
silver's for service, gold enduring worth;
home, family, hard work – both celebrate.
That silver spoon, unused, must tarnish fast.
Those rings will shine and last until the date
when one of you is laid in the dark earth.

6

In marriage, as elsewhere, you cannot give
offence, forgiveness, gifts, or a surprise! –
unless your partner is prepared – and tries –
to take, accept, receive or register
the proffer. You cannot possibly forgive
offenders who deny their fault. We live
by reciprocity: the marriage ties
are complementary. He answers her,
she him. They both prevail and each defer.

That's obvious – and that's the easy bit!
The hard bit is acceptance, care and trust,
the *act* of married love, which you each must
deliver unconditionally – for it
decides whether the marriage lives, or dies.

'First, for your children's procreation, then
to be a remedy for sin and wrong,
but most for mutual comfort for as long
as you both live together...' Once again,
I hear those dreadful words, and wonder when
our time will come. Each marriage is a song
which ends. Both partners must be brave and strong
to sing it, or survive in silence. Men
find marriage harder work than women do:
the widowed state is mostly female too.
Children and lust are challenges which fade,
as *they* grow up at last, and *you* grow old;
but loneliness is ever present. Hold
hands; learn to share and care; be unafraid.

Marriages totter — and they sometimes fall —
for three bad reasons: sex and kids and cash.
Sex is a game that grown-ups play: don't smash
the marriage, if your partner doesn't al-
ways play at home. You're there for the long haul.
Children are difficult, and parents clash
most often over childcare, make a hash
of loyalty, subjecting great to small:

partners come first, before the kids, before
your parents, siblings, self. That's what love means
in marriage. As for money, love of money
(the root of evil)'s a mistake: ignore
it. Focus on fidelity. It's funny:
just play your part — and skip the ugly scenes!

What works? Shared feelings, sharing dreams, a bath;
or choose some common goals. Shared enterprise
cements a marriage: projects, children ... Prize
the things you make and do together: hearth
and home, meals, humour, holidays – the lath
and plaster of a marriage. Exercise
and practise reciprocity: the wise
ones know that sharing smoothes the marriage-path.

Go for a walk together, learn to dance,
try out new restaurants, new films, hold hands:
you'll find familiarity enchants
(though novelty excites). True love expands
with practice: each true lover understands
good marriages are made, not left to chance.

What works? Accept, respect and celebrate
your difference. Observe the three degrees
of tolerance. Variety will please
the happy pair who learn to contemplate,
approve and praise the myriad ways their mate
is other than they are. They live at ease
together, well content that each one sees
and loves some different virtue, skill or trait.

Marriage demands a multitude of arts,
of which the first is patient listening;
the second – open-ended questions ('how
d'you feel about it?'); third – encouraging
each other to create what's in your hearts;
each passing moment focusing on *now*.

What works? – those loving words and kindly deeds
of marriage: smiles and kisses, holding hands,
poems and compliments and cards. Who reads
or hears, 'I love you, dearest!' understands
they hold in trust a treasure richer than
rubies, a gift more valuable than gold.
Who writes these words in faith, or speaks them, can
enjoy the fruits of love, as they grow old.
Good manners make strong marriages: so, keep
your word; be sure to put your partner first;
always apologise before you sleep:
of faults, not saying 'sorry' is the worst.
 Give praise, give thanks, give time, give help, forgive:
 you'll live in joy, as long as both shall live.

Marriages grow by stages: there are nine.
The first is wooing, next comes wedding, then
rehearsal of domestic skills – for when
the children come (the fourth, and finest). Wine
and marriages mature (or else decline)
gradually. The fifth phase is a test:
when partners contemplate their empty nest
and one another once more, some resign,
some stay together to enjoy stage six,
a shared Third Age, before their toughest trial,
the process of decay (phase seven) – while
bereavement marks the eighth. Once that is past,
the marriage still persists and lives in tricks
of memory: lone widowhood's the last.

13

Wooing is fun! – but focus on your aim:
you're looking for a long-term partner, not
a quick-change lover. While they share a lot
in common, they're by no means just the same –
like cheese and chalk: the first goes off soon (shame?
or a relief?), the other one has what
it takes to help you add that final dot
to your life's double portrait in its frame.

Choose carefully: remember that the art
of married love requires both heart and head.
So listen to the promptings of the heart
and mind. Sex matters; yet good marriages
are neither made in heaven, nor in bed,
but in acceptance, care, trust ... hers and his.

Often, a wedding ends a comedy,
and starts a tragedy, in Shakespeare's plays.
It's true that hard work follows holidays,
and after marriage life may seem to be
more serious, less frivolous and free.
But celebrate for now these special days
of parties, wedding, honeymoon; and raise
your glasses, and your hopes for harmony.

The wedding vows are speech-acts which transform
the speakers: nothing's ever quite the same
again – and nor are you. The rules of life
have changed: from now you play a different game.
Marriages bring new mindsets: they re-form
the words and deeds of wedded man and wife.

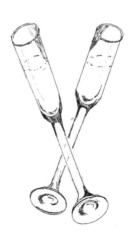

15

The third phase is the phoney war, before
the couple make a family. They play
at home-improvement, find some different way
to live together, try new roles, explore
the possibilities of marriage. More
seems intimate, less private, now that they
must share so much. Such intimacy may
test their commitment, rub their feelings raw.

Remember what you promised: keep your word.
This is a practice match; the major test
is still to come. So practise tolerance,
and practise trust. Mutual care is best.
Whatever contretemps may have occurred,
make love at home, not war. Kindness makes sense.

When children come, the marriage is full grown,
The partners, having learned to honour, each
the other, first, now learn that children teach
a tougher lesson: till the day they've flown
the nest of family, the children own
their parents. Freedom's now beyond your reach.
Henceforth your thoughts and actions show, your speech
reveals, a deeper care than you have known.

You learn that love will hurt in many ways:
when your beloved child is hurt, or when
that child hurts you, or when the precious days
of childhood pass, and you must learn to let
your children go, and live childless again –
with so much to remember, and forget.

After the children have grown up, and gone,
your lives and home and marriage seem to lose
their point and purpose for a time. Some choose
to end the marriage; others soldier on
to find new peace, as they set out upon
the sixth and sweetest stage of marriage. Use
your choice wisely: to leave home, or refuse
to pass across life's fatal Rubicon.

The best is yet to be, if you grow old
together. Trust yourselves. Renew your vows.
The silver marriage will transmute to gold.
The storm-clouds passed, the sun begins to shine
again. Enduring loyalty allows
you both a last sweet taste of summer's wine.

The golden sixth stage of a marriage lasts
as long as the Third Age of life allows.
Time pauses, while the evening sunlight casts
long shadows, warmth and kindness round you. Now's
the best part of the marriage, a reward
for perseverance, trust, hard work and care.
The mortgage paid, you've made your home; secured
a pension; learned to share and to forbear.
Grandchildren are the glory of this stage:
they fill your lives with joy, you theirs with love.
They give you hope and comfort in old age –
more true a future than in heaven above.
　　Hold hands, take care, keep faith – and you will see:
　　marriage improves with age, like poetry.

Decline precedes inevitable death.
Some weakness of the body, heart or mind
anticipates that final, fatal breath.
Demise is rarely quick, and seldom kind.
This is a testing time for both of you.
Patience is needed – patience to endure,
and patience to support the patient too.
Mortality's a sickness with no cure.
Acceptance, caring, trust (the *act* of love)
are more imperative than ever now.
The serpent's skill, the mildness of the dove,
are both required to help you keep your vow.
  For you must be companion, carer, nurse
  for one who's dying, weak – and getting worse.

And then one dies, released from pain and care.
The relict, left alone, endures the loss, the grief –
and guilt, since death so often gives relief
from duty. Now, no further need to share,
adapt and serve, to bear or to forbear.
The solitude of widowhood's the chief
sorrow bereavement brings, contentment's thief:
to live alone, who once formed half a pair.

And yet the marriage is still half alive.
The funeral, the wake, obituary
and distribution of possessions, all
conspire to help the partnership survive.
Widows and widowers are never free
from the remembered past, until they fall.

The loneliness of widowhood's the last
of the nine phases of a marriage. You
wake up alone, eat meals alone, and do
a thousand things alone that in the past
you did together. Years slide by so fast,
while hours drag slowly. Now (once one of two)
a singleton, the old marital glue
dissolved, your marriage finally has passed
away. And yet, the faithful wedding rings
remain in place, where they are often found
the day those relicts die. Marriage survives
in memory: it lives on all around
us: objects, children, grandchildren – those things
and thoughts and loved ones born of two joint lives.

Marriage is public: you each share a name
(Mr. and Mrs.), wear those wedding rings
and make your home together. Marriage brings
public responsibilities, the same
for each of you to bear. It is a game
(like Bridge) for partnerships to play. Nothing's
completely one's own business. Queens and kings
assume a role like this they can't disclaim.

Like kings and queens, you represent a state –
the state of matrimony. Marriage is
a social institution which secures
the fabric of society. The weight
of others' expectations is now yours:
your marriage safeguards other marriages.

Marriage is private: only partners know
what really happens in relationships –
the meaning in those gently-meeting lips,
the covert recognition each may show
the other at a party. Couples grow
closer, as marriages mature, like ships
moored beam to beam in harbour, whose sea-trips
are finished, now there's nowhere else to go.

The secretness of marriage is its charm:
Enjoy those private moments and the hours
of intimacy. Walking arm in arm,
or sleeping spoon-like in a velvet bed,
or knowing what the other's left unsaid –
these are the times when marriage blooms and flowers.

24

Marriage is memories – the unquiet past
a many-coloured patchwork, uncomplete
and fraying both at once, the sour and sweet,
the light and dark, a polychrome contrast
of feelings and events, some fading fast,
some still as clear as bold print on a sheet
of paper. Sadly, happy days retreat
from recall: it's the saddest ones that last.

Treasure those photo-albums, scrap-books, snaps
of smiling couples holding hands somewhere
now long-forgotten, children now full-grown –
the precious relics of the life you share.
These memories will comfort you, perhaps,
when, one day, you are widowed, and alone.

The silver wedding is the perfect time
to take stock of a marriage: what goes well,
and what does not. The children are your prime
concern – but not for long. The carousel
of marriage starts another circuit. Soon
you'll find yourselves alone again, and learn
whether, each night, each day, the same old tune
persuades you both to face another turn,
without distractions. We thought it worthwhile
to try again to find that secret door
to happiness, to learn to reconcile
ourselves to what we are – nor ask for more –
and celebrate together present, past,
and future, for as long as life might last.

26

Marriage is plans and projects, the unknown
future awaiting you in years to come:
a family, with you as Dad and Mum,
careers and learning, holidays, your own
dream-home to raise the children till, full-grown,
they fly the nest – and you develop some
new ventures on the long continuum
of marriage, where you're never quite alone –

until you're quite alone. Enjoy these plans,
designing different futures for your lives:
experiment with travel, gardening,
your own small business; learn to paint or sing.
Wise couples who become grandpas and grans
always remember: only one survives.

Make marriage an adventure: every year
do something different – grow tomatoes, dance,
adopt a child, explore another sphere
of life together, while you have the chance.

Go somewhere different – China or Peru.
Imagine future worlds, study the past,
visit Jerusalem, where Moslem, Jew
and Christian learn to make their marriage last.

Be someone different: try exchanging roles –
provider, carer; leader, follower;
the one who grieves, the other who consoles;
the speaker, and the patient listener.

Explore variety, take risks, behave
like *dramatis personae,* act! Be brave.

28

Enjoy familiarity. Each year
your marriage seems more settled, more secure.
You learn to care, accept and trust – more sure
of one another – as time passes. Where
you wondered once at strangeness, now the dear
familiar comfort of the known is your
reward. The prize for learning to endure
is learning to enjoy. You grow more near,
more reconciled, more faithful, more alike.
You almost seem like siblings, rather than
a married couple. Now you don't dislike
what once offended you so much. You learn
to love – by practising. Good practice can
feel good: good feelings yield good deeds in turn.

Marriage is funny – both in bed and out.
A sense of humour solves more things than rows
will ever solve. A smile or laugh allows
you both a breathing space, when fear and doubt
infect the partnership. Don't think about
lost love – it will return – or solemn vows,
forgotten amidst tears and wrinkled brows.
Comic relief always brings peace about.

Make fun of marriage – make the marriage fun!
Tell jokes (but not against each other). Tell
your partner something funny every day:
'*Your* man-flu and *your* headaches cancel one
another,' said the counsellor. 'No way!' –
the two agreed at last – and all was well.

Marriage is serious – more so than life
or death, since you've each promised faithfully
to render all you have, as man and wife,
one partner to the other, if need be.

This loyalty means more than worldly goods,
or body-service, though that's where you start;
nor is it just a list of *oughts* and *shoulds*.
It means a settled mind and faithful heart.

A marriage means commitment, day and night,
to one another, while forsaking all
distractions – errant sexual delight,
illicit love, temptations large and small.

Until you die, you dedicate your life,
as wife to husband, husband to your wife.

Nothing's more interesting than marriage is!
Friendship, or parenthood? – Neither compels
attention to the rich complexities
relationships reveal: marriage excels
in challenge, interest and benefit.
Friendship seems simple, parenthood too brief,
beside that subtle knot true lovers knit
in lifelong marriage – spun from joy and grief –
acceptance, care and trust – the qualities
successful couples learn to cultivate.
The compound interest of marriage is
that equal partnership of mate with mate.
    It starts the moment that you leave the church:
    a lifetime's study, trial and research.

Marriage is made of scrapbook memories:
the day she smiled, 'Of course, I'll marry you,
darling!' – the day he danced for joy (he knew
he'd won the dream-girl). Marriage is
measured by milestones: anniversaries,
birthdays and Christmas, holidays and new
beginnings – jobs and homes, or grandkids who
amuse old age with youthful fantasies.

Marriage is melody and harmony.
Discords resolved and passages complete,
the music modulates to find a key
that echoes earlier tones – old tunes repeat
themselves and recapitulate old themes,
revive young love, refresh shared hopes and dreams.

'Remember, wash yourself each night, each day!'
his mother said. She had a little book,
red, he recalled, like Chairman Mao's. They took
it on their honeymoon for fun, and lay
in bed together giggling at the way
it talked of sex and hygiene. As they look
back over sixty years – learning to cook,
to clean, to kiss – such skills still count today.

Women are better at these things than men.
They have more patience, drains and empathy.
They matter, when a marriage starts – and then
again towards the end (and in between!).
They are the faith and hope and charity
of marriage – but the greatest is: keep clean!

34

This is the one you've all been waiting for –
on sex! Sex is a game – of patience – played
by two intent on pleasure. Getting laid,
unless for procreation, has both pure
and impure motives: *intimacy* – more
for her than him; *relief* – albeit delayed –
for him, of course. But both may be betrayed
alike by cruel *possession*'s false allure.

She wants to have him – keep her precious prize.
He wants to have her – drain the glass and find
another bottle. Disown ownership!
But try to reach a balance, when you strip
for sex, between climax and closeness. Kind
lovers can lie together without lies.

The advent of a child is magical.
Conception is a mystery, but birth
you both remember as a wonderful
moment – perhaps the best of life on earth.

Born or adopted, children change our lives,
transform rash lovers into parents, make
fathers from husbands, mothers from young wives,
pierce them with love that never fails to ache.

Babies at birth all struggle to escape;
their childhood is one long continuous quest
for freedom, while prefiguring the shape
of things to come – your home an empty nest.

No sooner do you have your babies, than
you have to learn to lose them – if you can.

36

Parents learn more from children than they teach.
'Love me – and let me go!' they seem to cry –
and we, home-, cash-, and care-providers, try
to let them go, without an open breach.
You learn to disown ownership, as each
beloved nestling bravely learns to fly:
some glad to go, some sad, all go. (Some die.)
You die a bit, as they move out of reach.

Parental love is hard to learn, and harder still
to unlearn, as you must, if children are
to learn true independence. All your skill
and patience now is needed to translate
protective love to adult friendship – far
more difficult to do without a mate.

37

Those nestlings fledged, most couples think again
(we did) about their marriage: twist or stick?
We stuck together, as agreed, through thick
and thin: and now together we remain –
with no regrets, and much to do – come rain
or shine. The life that's left's an *Augenblick*
beside the life we've led. We must be quick,
before we're dead, to launch our last campaign.

We've had a good life: made our home, our pile,
our family. We've found the recipe
for happiness: some books and friends (both true),
service, achievement, creativity –
in each case freely chosen. Our last trial
will be to die a good death, when it's due.

38

And, once we're gone, what will remain of us?
Nobody's memory survives – beyond
two generations (say) – however fond
the family or friends may be. The fuss
of funerals, obituaries (plus
the legacies!) soon fades; the bond
of clear remembrance breaks. But don't despond:
not all the dead become anonymous.

We hope to live on in these poems and
these paintings. Only art survives for long.
Those few who labour with their mind and hand –
to build a pyramid, or write a play,
invent a story, or compose a song –
their names survive the passing of their day.

Bad marriages mean wasted lives – but make
good stories! Think of Hamlet's mother's, or
Othello's, the Macbeths, or *Lear*. The more
You study marital disasters – break-
ups, breakdowns, broken hearts and lives, mistake
or misrepair, the more you learn that poor
communication makes a marriage raw.
Words soothe a sore, and speech relieves an ache.

Ask gentle questions; learn to listen; talk
to one another; share your deepest dreams
and feelings, hopes and fears. A marriage needs
both time and tenderness, kind words and deeds
of love. Converse with care: that home truth seems
less harsh – while washing up, or on a walk.

Life without purpose is a waste of time:
an aimless marriage is no different.
Good partnerships invent, and re-invent,
a joint agenda – some new hill to climb,
shared skill to master, simple or sublime,
a project or a party ... Indolent
marriages make for mischief, discontent
and sin, as idle fingers turn to crime.

So, make a list each year of things to do
together – plan the wedding, paint a room,
conceive a child, move house, or join a choir,
take holidays abroad, learn something new
you both like, dance, or make your garden bloom ...
Connect, combine, co-operate, conspire.

Great vices mar, small virtues mend, a marriage.
If morals prove elusive, mind your manners.
When all seems lost, hurt partners won't disparage
polite behaviour, jeer at Pollyanna's
refusal to despair, or smash the crockery.
Small miracles are wrought by simple courtesy,
especially when the marriage seems a mockery.
Display some gentleness for him, or her, to see.
Betrayal stings; a slob is also vexious.
Say 'please' and 'thank you'; wash your hair and shave well –
good manners, like good humour, prove infectious.
Although you can't be good, at least behave well.
  Manners and marriage make a perfect pairing,
  like trust and truth, kindness and care – and sharing.

Should I compare it to a five-act play?
No. It's more precious, more elaborate
than some old *Winter's Tale* or *Dream* of May
or June – or anything that Shakespeare writ.
The Tempest is too fierce; *Love's Labour's Lost*
belies its value; neither comedy
nor tragedy – shepherds, Romans, star-crossed
lovers – can match its calm sublimity.
The beauty of a marriage will soon fade,
and be forgotten, when the partners die.
And if some hopeful poet may have made
a sonnet to preserve it – poets lie!
  Hamlet lives on: a marriage can't survive
  beyond the day its actors are alive.

The possibilities of marriage are
endless: a business or a family?
service, achievement, creativity?
a book, a school, a cruise? Follow your star
together; find some bold adventure, far
or near, to share. Joint projects are the key
to marital success and harmony.
Be more than just some ex-child's Pa and Ma.

Being Alongside, Learning, Loving (Sex!):
ideas like these inspired our marriage once –
initial letters of a common name
provide the starting-point for a great game! –
and still do. Here's the glue and sustenance
that saves you from becoming just an ex.

44

My partner wants a poem on *respect* –
a nuptial virtue hard to do without,
if both are to endure the days of doubt
and disappointment – which they must expect
in any lifelong marriage. The effect
of scorn is withering to love; puts out
the candle of concern; contempt's the drought
that kills kindness and confidence, unchecked.

So, never diss your partner, if you play
Duplicate Bridge, or share the discipline
of marriage. Mutual respect's a must –
essential, like acceptance, care and trust –
if those young, hopeful lovers who begin
the marriage, would sustain it all the way.

Marriage requires division of your labours.
We thought that each should lead and dominate
in different spheres of life. Negotiate
whose realm is family and friends and neighbours,
whose work and money. You'll find any way bores
you both in time, so re-negotiate,
experiment, swap functions with your mate.
Repetitive arrangements pall like Weber's.

It's best when both may choose the things they like,
and do well. Show restraint when planning who
should lead in areas, where both of you
are experts, both enjoy, both naturally
assume responsibility – for we
have found most problems where we're most alike.

Eldests who marry eldests face the danger
of similarity and competition.
Each seeks to dominate, as if their mission
were *winning* marriage. What is even stranger
are couples who adopt 'dog-in-the-manger'
poses – who spoil a partner's fair ambition,
as if they half believed the superstition
that life is best for the confirmed 'lone ranger'.

It's simple: partnership means nothing, if
the partnership does not take precedence
over the interests of the partners, who
have promised faithfully to share, the two
as one, life's varied good and bad events,
their joys and sorrows, home and handkerchief.

Pride, anger, envy, avarice and greed –
with lust and sloth: the seven deadly sins!
And seven is the number that you need
to list the faults of marriage: double gins,
and double chins; compulsive eating – shopping;
fault-finding, boasting, or making a scene,
a mess, a scandal; talking without stopping –
on second thoughts, it's more like seventeen! –
forgetfulness and laziness and lewdness,
incessant criticism, dirty hair,
disloyalty, self-righteousness and rudeness ...
Habits like these are difficult to bear!
    The list seems endless: focus, not on vice,
    but virtue. Try your hardest to be nice.

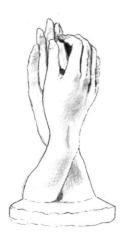

48

Learning the art of marriage is like dancing:
the one-step first – just walk around the floor
together – listen to the beat, advancing,
retreating, turning, promenade – before
you try the waltz's graceful *one-two-three*.
The Quickstep, Foxtrot, Rumba's *quick-quick-slow*
are harder still. They've quite defeated me!
(Those Latin dances – you don't want to know.)
Don't try to waltz until you've learned to walk.
In marriage, too, take one step at a time.
Don't risk a row until you've learned to talk.
Woo her in prose before you dare to rhyme.
   Dancing and marriage share a common style:
   hold hands, keep time, and move together. Smile!

49

You can't keep time. Time steals away, like joy
and hope and love – and life. A marriage dies.
Yourself, your partner, both – time must destroy:
one first, and then the other; close those eyes
for ever. I would rather be the dead
one, than survive a few more lonely years.
Marriage is mortal: couples who once wed
become unwed, when one life disappears.
Nothing remains but memories and grief.
Marriage begins and ends with flowers that fade.
A faithful marriage always seems too brief.
But death must come – even if long delayed.
   You can't keep time: time keeps on sliding by.
   Only now is. All marriages must die.

50

A Golden Wedding is a great achievement.
It proves the marriage has so far evaded
its natural enemies; divorce, bereavement.
And even if your golden hair has faded,
and mine is white, our smiles remain as kind,
our eyes as bright, our words as full of life,
as when, five decades past, we chose to bind
ourselves unbreakably as man and wife.
This is a day for friends and family.
Our children, and our grand-children, were there.
This was a day for them, and us, to see
the fruits of tolerance, of trust and care.
  We will remember gladly, whilst we may,
  the triumph of our Golden Wedding day.

51

Enjoy the present, celebrate the past –
if you can still remember it – and plan
that future of your dreams, while you yet can.
The autumn of your marriage will not last
for long; September's warmth is fading fast.
It feels like yesterday it first began.
But, like the dying year, your marriage-span,
for better or for worse, will soon have passed.

It's not too late to mend the marriage: love
your partner! First forgive – and then forget –
their faults; accept them as they are; above
all else, respect them; offer care and trust.
The hard part's this: there is no deal. You must
take what you get – for true love claims no debt.

52

The poetry of marriage is not free
expression, self-indulgent sloppy verse.
It's disciplined – for better or for worse,
the marriage-lines have due formality.
Good marriages are like *The Odyssey*,
long, episodic, challenging, diverse
(unlike an epigram or haiku – neat and terse)
epics – with heroes, culture, dynasty:

not measureless, not formless (like *Ulysses?*),
but structured, formal, shapely, like sestinas.
(The apple goes to Juno, not to Venus,
in marriage.) Yes. The more I muse upon it,
the more convinced I have become that this is
what wedlock's like: the strict Italian sonnet.

53

And so the next one follows Shakespeare's style,
who wrote a gross or more dissecting love,
extolling his dark lady's eyes or smile,
in rhymes I'm sometimes tempted to reprove.
His subject is not mine. He paints the lover
prostrated by a passion which he knows
he never can – we know he will – recover
from: I portray the partners – those who chose
the discipline of marriage, those who choose
each day, each night, to reconfirm that choice,
and in the service of their marriage use
their every skill and strength, head, heart, hand, voice.
  They hold the secret of a happy life:
  the marriage of a kind man and good wife.

54

Sonnets, like marriage, rarely work in threes —
rhymed lines or partners linked in harmony.
One of them always feels anomalous.

Couplets, like couples, match and mate. They please
the ear and eye, the heart and mind, while three
seem clumsy, tasteless — like an octopus,

or triphthongs, or three-legged races. These
trios — triplets — triangles may well be
useful in maths or music: not for us —

unless the mistress or the lover's just
for sex (as third lines add comic effect!).
But, even then, in bed or verse, you must
be careful. Few love-poets can protect
all readers from some feelings of disgust

The exception to this rule is *terza rima,*
in verse: in marriage, when the third's your child.
A child may be the marriage's redeemer.
Partners who row are sometimes reconciled
as parents, while Dante's great epic proves
the Trinity is blest (and sin defiled).
What life bestows, death equally removes:
a lost child is a tragedy – and trial.
No marriage moves in predetermined grooves.
Life sometimes makes us grieve, and sometimes smile.
The challenge is to treat both just the same,
and walk with measured feet that extra mile
of marriage, always faithful to your aim,
like Dante's dreamer facing hell's dark flame.

Perhaps the patient reader feels they've heard
enough of this analogy between
marriage and metrical arrangements. Verse
is rich with meaning, but a marriage counts
for more with those involved, the partners, friends
and family, for whom the marriage makes
an anchor to their lives. Great poetry's
remembered longer than good marriages –
though the reverse is true with bad mistakes,
both metrical and marital. Who spends
more time and effort? Spouses. What amounts
to full-time love, for better or for worse,
life-long, is their commitment. (Verse has been
a part-time job since Poe.) Each gives their word.

57

What gift, once given, must be kept? Your word.
Integrity means nothing more than this,
and nothing less. Then, practise kindliness.
These are the first and second rules. The third,
a triple rule, is one you've often heard
before: the *act* of marriage – never miss
a chance – accept and care and trust. A kiss
works wonders, when hard words are best deferred.

Always apologise before you sleep.
Always forgive the errant partner who
is truly contrite, even if untrue.
Wise spouses seek to understand: the fool
rushes to judgement. Follow the first rule:
your word is what you give – and what you keep.

58

We wrote a list of things that make us sad,
or mad: the bad behaviours that can spoil
a marriage – lateness, lying, less than loyal
support, not listening ... and I might add
both laziness and lechery. (I'm glad
we limited the list to L!) Our royal
rows often come when little things embroil
us in dispute. We act the cat, and cad.

Contentedness and cleanliness and calm
enhance a marriage. Learning how to cope
with disappointment, disagreement, days
of boredom or temptation, can disarm
a nuptial duel, and divert a blaze
of anger. Trust in humour, hygiene, hope.

Children need time and talk and tenderness.
And so does marriage. There's no substitute
for time: this is the ground in which the fruit
and flower of marriage grow. Those partners miss
the truth who claim that cash gives nuptial bliss.
Talk is the air the slender marriage-shoot
must breathe to live – and listening. The root
needs rain, the tender tears of kindliness.

For tenderness and talk and time provide
the recipe for marital success –
endurance, tolerance and happiness.
These qualities and practices will guide
the married couple through life's complex maze
to Silver, Gold and Diamond Wedding days.

A Diamond Wedding is a rarity.
Neither our parents, nor grandparents, nor
(I guess) their forbears, ever reached three score
years of a marriage. With our family,
we celebrate today: when will there be
another such occasion? I am sure
they'll have to wait for many years before
a second nuptial Diamond Jubilee.

Perhaps not. For we like to think that what
we have achieved may help encourage others:
our children, grandchildren, our sisters, brothers,
friends, witnesses, to run the marathon
of marriage like us – keep on keeping on –
to win the rich rewards that we have got.

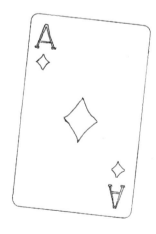

These five – health, wealth and happiness, the love
of virtue, destiny fulfilled – comprise
a Chinese blessing. But, not from above
flow blessings, raindrops falling from the skies.

You have to help them grow. Marriages work,
provided partners both work at them. This
five-pointed blessing's not for those who shirk
hard work. Marriage needs more than one quick kiss.

Health, wealth and happiness go hand in hand.
Couples who play together stay together.
Plan what to do, and do the things you planned.
Remember, when it rains, you made the weather.

Couples who study the philosophy
of marriage will fulfil their destiny.

62

The marital philosophy I like
is simple wisdom: first, make promises;
then, keep them. Understand the contract is
quite clear: you can't go slow, can't go on strike,
cannot resign – although you may dislike
the terms from time to time. Most marriages
are chequered; most nuptial fidelity's
partial; most partners do not take a hike.

Sexual fidelity is over-rated.
Adultery is a bad habit, rather
like farting, but should not be a deal-breaker.
That love-affair, which might have devastated
your marriage, was short-lived: real love goes farther –
the lifelong love that is the marriage-maker.

63

And so, at last, you come to harmonise
like those two violins that Bach composed
his great Double Concerto for – that rise
and fall of married melody, enclosed
in graceful harmony – celestial sound,
unwinding, twining, kind and sweet and slow,
until the music is at last unwound,
and each rapt player lays aside their bow.
Celestial music sometimes lingers in
the mind and heart. Good marriages remain
in memory a while – and then they're gone,
forgotten, lost. But others venture on
the quest of marriage to release again
that music latent in each violin.

64

And yet, disharmony is never far
away. The habit of dissatisfaction
is hard to bear: the natural reaction
(of irritation) harder still. These are
some challenging behaviours which can mar
a happy marriage, and transform attraction
into repulsion Quick! Get into action
before such problems leave a lasting scar.

We can unlearn our learned behaviours; learn
new ways of being; choose to be content,
or patient; jointly practise self-restraint.
The prize is worth the effort: we may earn
the rich reward of nuptial peace. What mayn't
they win, who learn to lose the argument?

65

Successful marriage is an art you learn
(or not) through trial and error, after years
of study and research. Few couples earn
their doctorate in marriage without tears
and laughter, tantrums and apologies,
trouble and compromise. Marriage is more
(much more!) complex than rocket-science is,
more delicate than brain-surgery or
poetry. Patience, yes, and fortitude
(as Kingsley claimed) – and luck – are what you need
to keep the girl you wooed, the boy who wooed
you, as the years of married life proceed.
　　Your marriage must, to prove successful, be
　　made fresh each morning – like a cup of tea.

A kiss, a cup of tea, a compliment;
a smile, attention, or a nice surprise
(like sex, or flowers); 'thank-you' said, and meant;
such acts of grace should be one's daily exercise.
Grace is the friend of marriage; gracelessness
its foe – the tempter leading to disgrace,
distress, divorce. Kindness provides the kiss
of life to marriage, yielding time and space
for reconciliation after rows,
and compromise in place of confrontations.
Marriage responds to kindness, more than vows,
or tears, or silence, or long explanations.
 Remember: marriages require (above
 all else) countless small acts of grace and love.

Behaviour is habituated choice.
Choose marriage-habits with especial care:
the way you raise the children, or your voice
to criticise your partner, whinge, or swear.
Repeated patterns of behaviour stick
like chewing-gum adhering to a shoe –
anxiety, or alcohol: a quick
temper, or failing to clean up the loo …
The list of marital offences is
a long and sad one. Practise better ways
of being: keep your word (integrity's
a must), and hold your peace (endurance pays).
  Honour your marriage, and your mutual choice,
  to make it one in which you both rejoice.

68

The process of creation of a child,
or of the world, is what religion, and
what sex, are all about. That's why the brand-
new marriage starts in church, and bed. God smiled
on Sunday; parents smile together, mild
as milk, to see the baby they have planned.
Partners in marriage come to understand
that through creation all is reconciled.

Sex and religion dwindle over time –
become mere recreations, pastimes, play,
once we have consummated procreation
and found this godless world is still sublime.
But marriage never is mere recreation:
It must be recreated every day.

The married couple quickly learn to share –
a bed, the children, washing-up, a laugh.
What works best's often not exactly fair.
Good sharing isn't always half and half.

Division of your labour – Adam Smith's
idea – works just as well in marriage as
the workplace. Don't believe the modern myths
of strict equality – and all that jazz.

Another kind of sharing's taking turns.
Your joint agenda grows from common goals:
one keeps the home you share, the other earns
the living that is shared. (You might change roles.)

The subtle art of marriage-sharing must
be grounded in acceptance, care and trust.

A lifelong marriage is a process, not
a project – more like growing old than growing
potatoes. Value lies in the ongoing
experience more than the outcome. What
you must remember is that life's a lot
more shaped by *being* than by doing, knowing,
or having things. Be calm, be kind, keep going;
persistence more than purpose seals the knot.

Good marriage, like good poetry, exists –
and that's enough. There's no *in order to*,
no goal beyond – the poet's and – your joint
commitment to ensure that it persists,
for better or for worse, until the point
when certain death has widowed one of you.

The wedding-partners separately choose
to live together through the years to come.
Once married, they will choose together some
of what most helps a marriage keep, or lose,
serenity: their home, the children, views
and friends and holidays. A Dad and Mum
who march to music from a different drum
hear doleful music, sounding like the blues.

Shared choices in a marriage are a must.
You must choose children's names together, for
example, or who sleeps on either side
of your shared bed, or when to make love, or
peace, or the bed. Shared choice requires real trust
in two joint lives, where love means more than pride.

Words matter: what you say can make, or break,
the marriage. Watch your mouth and guard
  your tongue.
A curt remark or casual insult, flung
across the room, can swell in memory, and ache
like rotting teeth. Bad words are a mistake
like bad behaviour, or bad breath. Among
the things that make us glad are thoughts of young
love's language, soft as ripples on a lake.

So, wash your mouth out, clean your teeth, and floss,
each day, each night. And practise gratitude
and compliments. Ask the best question you'll
ever receive or tender since you wooed
each other once, without a thought of loss:
how can I make your life more wonderful?

The terminology of marriage is
quite simple. You need only three or four
key terms at most: the usual courtesies
(of course) of *please* and *thank you*, and one more –
a word that's more important even than
sorry, and much more difficult to say.
A couple's blest, when both the partners can
reciprocate this magic word each day.
What is it? No, it's not *I love you*, though
it's not a bad idea to practise this
key phrase, provided you take care to show
you mean it – and confirm it with a kiss.

   It's *yes*. The marriage will not thrive unless
   both partners bravely practise saying, 'Yes'.

74

A cruel conjuror, age makes us look
and live – whether or not we liked them – like
our parents. As time riffles through the book
of life, the generations look alike,
sound similar and act in the same way.
So, study one another's parents when
you woo – how they behave and what they say.
They show the shape of things to come – again!
You find you're marrying a family,
not just one special person, when you marry.
Mothers-in-law reveal how brides may be,
and why your precious marriage might miscarry.
　　Keep faith! The secret of success is just
　　the magic of acceptance, care and trust.

You have to love, you do not *have* to like,
each other – though it helps. Feelings like these
are *chosen*: love and liking (or dislike)
are options. We can think what thoughts we please,
in principle, and feel the way we choose.
It makes good sense to choose to like your wife
(or husband) – otherwise you find you lose
your love, and spoil the marriage – and your life.
Love's a commitment, once you've made the choice
to marry. Marriage offers no back door
or fire-escape. You may as well rejoice
in mutual love, since mutual hate's a bore.
  A loving marriage is a rich resource –
  essential, if you seek a good divorce!

I wonder why they don't teach choice in school?
Choices are promises you freely make
first, to yourself; then, others. If you break
a promise, or reverse a choice, the rule
requires you to clear up the mess. And you'll
not find that easy! It's a bad mistake
to void a vow, betray a choice. Heart-ache
and headaches follow, and the costs are cruel.

The marriage-vow's a choice. The wedding band
binds both of you. The marriage will be eased
if each of you has chosen to be pleased
with what you've jointly chosen, and rejoice
as well at the inevitable – and
the unintended – consequence of choice.

One hundred, and then fifty, and then four
more sonnets William Shakespeare wrote to make
a living in a year when plague once more
had closed the theatres in Town. I take
some comfort from the thought this one's half way
towards his total. But I wonder how
long his great sonnet-sequence took him? Say,
he had a few already done; allow
nine months or so – it still means three a week!
I think that poetry's a craft you must
practise, like marriage – not just wait and seek
for inspiration. We all come to dust.
  In marriage, as in verse, the glass, the dial,
  the book, each tell the time, brook no denial.

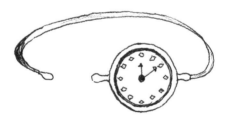

Their marriage is a puzzle: Will away
in London, writing plays and acting, Anne
in Stratford, raising children, home-bound. They
bought a grand home fit for a gentleman –
New Place – how often did he visit it,
I wonder? Think of all those sonnets penned
to some Dark Lady: could Anne read his wit
and wisdom, and not mind? Did he intend
an insult with that strange bequest – a bed
(and not the best one in the house)? I guess,
perhaps, she grew feeble ... Judith, instead,
(their daughter) ran the house and business.
    All marriages are mysteries: so do
    not judge – lest one day someone judges you!

The Marriage Guidance Council (now *Relate*)
tells us what causes marital decay:
sex, cash – children, of course – affairs; but way
beyond these – failing to communicate.
It pays to talk, and listen, to one's mate:
say something to each other every day!
The fabric of a marriage starts to fray
when partners choose to live in silent hate.

Say something kind – a compliment; or ask
how she, or he, is feeling; gratitude
is never a mistake; you might enquire
how you could help, or if there's some small task
you might perform. Avoid advice, or rude
remarks. Exchange 'good-nights', when you retire.

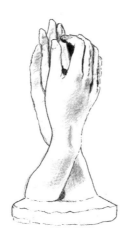

Practise communication: words and smiles
and kisses; cards and gifts and courtesies.
Hold hands, hold fast, hold on. A marriage is
a marathon – and you have many miles
to go. Small kindnesses soften the trials
and upsets of relationships, and *his*
embrace, or *her* response, are remedies
like water for a thirst. Love reconciles.

Practise the stern vocation of your state –
for marriage is a true vocation, like
the poet's and the priest's. You dedicate
your lives to service, faithfulness and art –
performance art. Most marriages are not unlike
good dramas: learn your lines, and play your part.

Dramatic marriages include Jocasta
(with Oedipus) and Clytemnestra's to
King Agamemnon, Nora's – I've amassed a
long list of failed relationships for you:
Hermione's or Desdemona's, or
(indeed) most literary marriages.
In plays or novels partners are at war,
provoking pain and anguish, hers and his.
Must life reflect the realm of literature –
since literature's supposed to mirror life?
Where is the model to make him, or her,
the ideal husband or the patient wife?
    Forget the stories; make your marriage strong
    by acting as if nothing's ever wrong.

Though talk is healthy, talking-over's bad —
both in and out of marriage. *Listening's*
an under-rated skill, which makes us glad;
while interruption irritates and stings
like wasps or nettles — and the pains persist
long after the wrong-doer's quite forgotten
the fault. Resist it, as wise men resist
asking their wives, 'Whatever have you got on?'
There is a deficit in people's lives
of patient, kind attention: 'Tell me more;
that sounds so hard; how are you feeling?' Wives
and husbands who 'talk over' are at war.
  While speech is silver, silence is pure gold:
  good listening provides rewards untold.

U*xorious* – strange word! It signifies
a man's 'submissive or excessive love'
towards his partner. I would not advise
the hawk as model for a marriage: dove-
like gentleness is what you need, both man
and wife. It's odd there's no word *maritorious
for wives who love their spouse more fondly than
they should: we lack a converse to *uxorious*.
And anyway, how can you love too much?
Love is like marriage, or a pregnancy,
not more or less, but yes or no. And such
is marriage that you both must bend the knee.
 Language misleads. Select your words with care.
 Wise partners learn to trust, accept, and share.

84

He says:

I watch you leaving in your queenly gown,
and wonder when I'll see you re-appear
to fill the house with garden-colours. Here,
without your presence, life feels grey and brown –
like autumn after summer's blaze dies down,
when flowers fade, and fall, and winter's near.
You are the springtime in my life, my dear!
These lilies welcome your return from Town.

Queenlily, you re-enter your domain,
the home you've made, the marriage you sustain.
Accept this tribute from a husband, wife,
rejoicing in your love and care and art.
Accept the worship of my subject heart.
You are the queen and lily of my life.

She says:

My love is realised in work, not words.
I tend our garden, cook the meals, and sew.
(Interminable twitter's for the birds!)
When will you learn? Love me, and let me go.
My life lies all around me, not within.
Your introspection's not my cup of tea.
Surfaces please: why peer beneath the skin?
I can't be married, if I can't be free!
I want you to be free to live your life –
and I want the same freedom to live mine.
It's what she does, not says, that makes a wife.
And now – a cup of tea would be divine!
  (I'm glad you liked the dress: it took me hours
  to finish it – and thank you for the flowers!)

They say:

The secret is to make the differences
a source of pleasure for the pair of you.
Since that (we hope!) must certainly be true
of sex, and all the physicalities
of male and female, why (we wonder) is
the difference of attitude of two
people what may dissolve the superglue
of marriage, and augment its miseries?

Delight in difference, and learn to like
'the other' in the other person. They
fit best together, who are least alike.
Trust in that misquotation from La France,
that *tout comprendre, c'est tout pardonner*;
or, put more neatly, *vive la différence*.

Established marriages yield benefits
that sometimes come as a surprise – like snow.
or rainbows. Golden-married couples know
companionable silence; whilst she knits,
he reads. In bed, familiar intimates,
accepting the inevitable slow
retreat of passion and desire, they grow
together as contented celibates –

most nights. At last they've learned to celebrate
each other's virtues, and to tolerate
each other's vices. Both accept what can't
be changed: grey hair, false teeth and glasses aren't
so hard – but who can welcome, with a kiss
and smile, her worries, his forgetfulness?

Established marriages can be infected
with bad, habitual and shared behaviour –
like bickering, or finding fault. Connected
by mutual contempt, you'll soon deprave your
mutual vows of love and loyalty.
The misdemeanours of a marriage might
(like inattention or dependency)
appear less serious, but they (too) blight
the hopes of happiness you vowed to share.
Practise integrity (make promises
and keep them); trust, respect, acceptance, care –
remember these essential courtesies.
    Couples conspire to spoil their married life:
    but either one can save it, man or wife.

We met a pair – the wife had lost her past.
Without the past, the present makes no sense,
and what's to come is quite unknown, (The last
infirmity's not lust for fame!) Non-sense
is not endurable. (Death brings relief.)
Her husband lost his partner – but he found
a role, her lifelong care and comfort. (Grief
is selfishness.) One drowned, one run aground.
What qualities are needed for these parts?
For her, obedience, patience, sweetness, trust;
for him, good humour, duty. A kind heart's
essential – sympathy of mind a must.
  She had become his pet, a man's best friend.
  Shall we become like this before the end?

90

Babies and pets and those of feeble mind
have common needs – food, water, toileting,
sleep, grooming, exercise ... This sort of thing
is obvious: what's not – how to be kind?
Use statements and commands: such creatures find
questions too hard to answer; smile and sing;
stroking, approval, little treats will bring
relief, and help the patient to unwind.

Dumb animals and infants, the demented,
are often anxious. They can't understand
what's going on, which makes them discontented.
Our confidence is comforting: just tell
them, while you stroke their head, or hold their hand,
that all is well, and all things shall be well.

They grow accustomed – to his voice – her face,
the way she wears her hair – his sense of fun
and seriousness of purpose (any pun
or project pleases him) – her natural grace
in action or repose. He likes to chase
ideas – she cares for plants and people. One
lives in a world of words – things to be done
engage the other. Each has their own space.

And yet they're interlaced, these separate lives –
interdependent, like the sea and land –
like spooning couples – table forks and knives.
Dependency is dangerous: the hand
you hold still feels as warm, kind, quick – until
the day you find it cold, unfeeling, still.

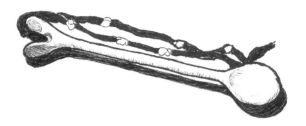

92

Long-distance marriages astonish me –
couples who practise partnership apart,
who somehow learn to consummate the art
of love by letter, telephone, IT.
Do words and pictures have such power? Maybe.
Our fingers need to feel the beating heart
of love, not trace a line across a chart.
I marvel at *their* calm and constancy.

Yet distance does not damage other kinds
of love – fraternal, friendship, filial.
Long separation can't untie what binds
parents and children, siblings, friends. So, why
is marriage different? Must I reply:
sex is the most important thing of all?

I doubt it. Sex is an expression of
true intimacy, not the thing itself.
The emblematic sign of married love
is intimacy – sharing self with self
without restraint, or hesitation, or
fear, both in bed and out, in age as youth,
in silence and in words, unceasing for
as long as both shall live in troth and truth.
An intimate relationship reveals
those sterling qualities these verses praise:
respect, acceptance, care and trust. Each feels
the other's feelings, holds the other's gaze.
   If I am wrong (and you can prove I am),
   I'll write no more – and marriage is a sham!

It's not, of course. Marriage is one of man's
(or woman's?) great inventions, like the wheel
or writing. Progress, proving an ordeal
for some, provides real benefit – which stands
the test of time – for most of us. The bands
of wedlock chafe the ones who *choose* to feel
constrained. Calligraphy and oil will heal
a squeaky wheel, reform those ill-formed hands –

and honesty and honour may amend
a messy marriage, if the partners choose
to clean it up. A marriage is a *choice*
made daily. Faithfulness means you refuse
to contemplate failure, decline to voice
dismay, and persevere until the end.

Friendship is good, sex better, marriage best –
since marriage offers friendship-with-sex, and
a good deal more besides. You'll find you're blest,
once you learn self-reliance – how to stand
on your own feet; twice blest, once you have learnt
to care for others – children, parents – thrice
blest in an equal partnership. Wives weren't
their husbands equals once: we've scotched that vice –
marriage as slavery – the wife oppressed,
the husband power-corrupted. Whilst it's slow,
progress is sure – and marriage has progressed,
as every equal wife today must know.
  Marriage must be a loving partnership.
  Life's longest journey is a one-way trip.

Dealing with Breakdown's a whole chapter in
'The Art of Marriage'. First, you welcome it:
a breakdown, while demanding delicate
treatment, is where a breakthrough may begin.
Start with apology. Aim, not to win
a war, but make the peace; and try to knit
a new relationship, more intimate;
a marriage more secure through thick and thin.

Bring listening and love to breakdowns. Bring
kindness and care. Say sorry – nothing more.
Remember why you wear those endless bands
of gold, and never take them off. Hold hands.
Be silent. Make a small peace offering ...
The marriage may prove stronger than before.

In marriage you must share the things you own.
With all my worldly goods I thee endow:
a joint account might satisfy that vow,
but assets, as the passing years have shown,
mean more than money. We have always known
that time is precious too; good projects now
enrich our lives; and we are learning how
love comforts us – though each must die alone.

Real wealth is fivefold: culture, cash and care;
a rich agenda and a store of time.
The marriage means the two of you must share
these worldly goods to make a perfect rhyme
of the relationship. This is true wealth:
these are the means of happiness and health.

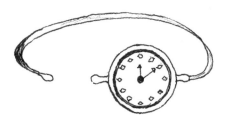

98

All marriages must end in death, divorce –
or disappointment. This is patent truth.
But few of us foresee the end, of course,
prancing along the primrose path of youth.
Death chooses us. Divorce is what we choose –
and disappointment, too. Each slow, sad stain
seems permanent, indelible: we lose
as much, or more, than all we hoped to gain.
Be very careful, then, if either choice
seems tempting: Satan can seduce in two
ways – both the active and the passive voice.
Rash acts, resentment, each engenders rue.
   Integrity works best: the wise choose death,
   keep faith, hold fast, until that final breath.

Unless they're missing, people tend to take
for granted things that really matter in
their lives, like health and wealth, or kith and kin,
their home and happiness – and marriage. Make
time for, peace with, love to, your partner! Wake
her with a kiss and cup of tea: begin
each day by thanking him. The medicine
of grateful service soothes the sorest ache.

Each month be brave enough to ask them what
they'd like – and generous enough to give
what's sought. Learn to say *yes*, not *we'll see*, not
some indirect (or direct) negative.
Learn the four words that loosen any knot
for her or him – *forbear, forget, forgive.*

Just *learn to love*, the poet wrote, *and leave*
all other things to be the way they are.
The core curriculum of marriage – far
more fundamental than most may conceive –
is love. Love's not in thought or feelings: weave
a web of loving *being, doing*. Star-
crossed lovers from the stage and cinema
delude themselves: love's failure's why they grieve.

Love gives, love bears, love smiles, love listens, love
makes promises – and keeps them. Love is strong.
Love lives in the distinction: *nothing's wrong*.
While never lovey-dovey, love's a dove
of peace, and dwells in care and courtesy.
Love offers unreserved apology.

The partners in the *Book of Genesis*
are parables – if not exemplars: Eve
and Adam; Noah and his wife; don't miss
Sarah, who laughed when told she would conceive
a second son for Abraham; or Lot,
with his rash wife, who turning turned to salt;
Rebekah, Isaac's wife; and Jacob (not
one wife, but two – Leah, whose only fault
was plainness, and young Rachel, who was fair);
and, lastly, Joseph – Joseph's wife's a blank,
although she gave him sons, another pair
whose destiny reversed the rules of rank.
  These seven marriages remind us why
  this Book was made – to guide and edify.

Adam and Eve come first: I read their tale,
not as a case of disobedience,
but self-reliance. They each had the sense
to take responsibility – and fail
(if adult life's a failure?) in this vale
of joy and tears on their own terms. Events
occur in life and marriage: both expense
and gains are ours. Complaining won't avail.

I value our first parents' enterprise,
resilience – and their endurance. Yet
their words are less than satisfactory.
Responsible behaviour must comprise
both act and owned responsibility.
I wonder if those words caused them regret?

103

Old Noah was a good man, but his wife
was just a wife, who gave him those three sons,
for nothing more is known of her long life.
After the Flood he took to drink, and one's
sorry for her, wedded to the first lush.
Tradition says she turned into a scold.
A husband with a habit might well crush
all kindness, so that love grows cold.
Or did she drive him to it? No one knows.
Unhappy marriages are hard to read,
like modern poetry or mannered prose.
What magic makes those floods of tears recede?
  Forget the fading rainbow, fragile dove –
  trust in the healing powers of human love.

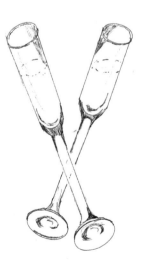

104

Incest and sodomy were commonplace
in those days. And they are today – why not,
assuming unconstrained consent? For Lot
slept with his daughters to produce a brace
of tribes. The pair from whom the chosen race
descends, Sarah and Abraham, were got
by the same father. Should we copy what
the Bible seems to teach – in every case?

Lot's wife's a puzzle. Like Eurydice,
she looked back (longingly?) towards the sins
of those two cities in the plain – and she
perished. Should we, when married life begins
to pall, and we are yearning to be free,
attempt to keep our vows – to save our skins?

Sarah and Abraham deserve a verse
all of their own. Sarah's a model wife,
who understood 'for better or for worse',
and loved her man throughout her long, hard life.
Devoted to his mission, Abraham
gave little thought to Sarah's wants or needs –
shared her with other men, claiming 'I am
her brother,' – childless, past her monthly bleeds ...
She gave her word, her maid, her son –
after the miracle of Isaac's birth –
to help him finish what he had begun.
But, once she'd died, he realised her true worth.
   Our lives are made for love, however brief:
   love now, for death turns love unshared to grief.

106

The key events in Isaac's life were all
arranged by others: birth, of course, and death –
after twice ninety years of life! Recall
the story of the child holding its breath
as Abraham prepared the sacrifice,
before the angel came to save his life.
His father's servant paid the bridal price
and led Rebekah home to be his wife.
And she it was arranged for Jacob to
supplant his elder, Esau, and receive
old Isaac's blessing, now half-blind. But who
knows what a life of patience may achieve?
    We praise the active life: but don't disparage
    the patient life – a virtue in a marriage.

The 'JACOB rule' requires you to eschew
Judgement, Advising, Criticism, or
Opinions – also Blame – or maybe you
should just try not to voice these 'threats of war'!
(Jacob by cunning stole his brother's place,
birthright and blessing; father of twelve sons,
and husband of two wives, he had a brace
of concubines besides – like Solomon's,
but fewer. Nonetheless, Yahweh was pleased
and blessed him with a new name – ISRAEL.
Divine displeasure's easily appeased
by God's chosen!) Marriage demands – above
all else – Integrity, Service as well,
Respect, Acceptance, Empathy, and Love.

Joseph comes last of all the patriarchs
recorded in the *Book of Genesis*.
You know the story: multi-coloured coat,
exile to Egypt, prison, Pharaoh's right-
hand man, his brothers reconciled, long life,
and longer legacy in Holy Writ.
His wife, who stayed at home to sew and knit
(I guess) – he married an Egyptian wife –
was called Asenath, daughter of a quite
important priest named Potiphera: note
how close it sounds to Potiphar! Was this
one family? Perhaps the marriage marks
another reconciliation. We
might learn how marriage can cure enmity.

Or cause it? Modern marriage is as apt
to start a war, as end it. The Divorce
Courts demonstrate this daily, since the course
of married love is rarely smooth. Those trapped
and tearful partners, who will not adapt,
adjust, accept or trust, suffer remorse
or – worse – self-righteousness, a certain source
of grief. A rigid stem is soonest snapped.

Read the Beatitudes – then follow them:
you build the marriage on a rock, not sand.
Your partnership becomes the ampersand
in *meek & mild*, or *give & take*: a gem
more precious as time passes – silver, gold,
then diamond – whilst together you grow old.

Does marriage have a moral purpose? What
a question! Modern life has largely lost
its sense of purpose – to our social cost.
But 'good enough is good enough' is not
a recipe for wedded bliss. The knot
you've tied demands commitment – fingers crossed,
maybe – to excellence. Although storm-tossed,
a marriage is a treasure-freighted yacht.

Your treasure is yourselves – your children, too –
those dear grandchildren – and their children: but,
beyond your family, your marriage is
a beacon, an example. Others you
affect, for no one's eyes and hearts are shut.
We copy virtues – and iniquities.

Divorce and driving, drink and drugs and debt,
gambling and guns, getting and spending, are
all correlates of crime. The private car –
with alcohol and drugs, a gun, a bet –
tempt weaker souls to sin. The strong forget
their role in normalising things that mar
the lives of others. I wonder how far
duty extends – to meet this social threat?

Divorce is damaging – to children and
to adults. We must never normalise
it. The exceptions prove – they don't disprove –
the rule that marriage is for life, for you've
each made a heart-deep promise, hand in hand,
to keep your word – till one or other dies.

A couple is convenient for sex
and conversation, Contract Bridge and care:
reciprocated care provides a neat
solution to the human need for love
both for and from another. Nothing wrecks
a marriage faster than when love's unfair,
unshared, unbalanced. Couples are complete:
the relict's an odd sock, an unmatched glove.
Widows and widowers find life's long trek's
a solitary pilgrimage to where
extinction lies. Until that last retreat
they live with silence, care-less, hoping dove-
like Patience takes the place of Duplicate.
Their sex is solo – or they're celibate.

I like to study settled marriages,
those partnerships that seem like deeds well done,
worthy and whole: each one a paragon
of faithfulness and love, where *hers* and *his*
mean *theirs*, where melody and harmonies
create the perfect cadence. Is there one –
in literature or life – I wonder? None
I know of is devoid of weaknesses.

The secret is to aim at excellence,
in full acceptance of our human state
of fallibility. Forgive, not once,
nor twice, but countless times; apologise
as often, since these subtle skills comprise
the toolkit of the marital estate.

114

What happened? *Sex with someone else.* So what
exactly did you make it mean? *My mate
has hurt me, meant to hurt me, loves me not ...*
... which justifies your anger, grief and hate?
Marriage is made of sterner stuff than this.
Adultery is gross discourtesy –
and nothing more. A stolen fuck or kiss
requires forgiveness (with apology).
Learn the hard lesson that your feelings are
your own responsibility – and no
one else's – for betrayal's lasting scar
is self-inflicted, seasoned partners know.
   A marriage is too precious to destroy
   because one partner chose forbidden joy.

The value of a marriage grows with age –
paper and cotton, silver, ruby, gold ...
What young ones take for granted fills the old
with gratitude. Like songbirds in a cage,
they sing more sweetly as that sad last stage
of life approaches. You may see them hold
each other's hands, before they're stiff and cold.
Good books get better on the final page.

And who may estimate the worth of what
a couple's life together has achieved?
Patient domestic heroism's not
much celebrated in the press or by
the poets, more's the pity. We should try
to praise these pairs *before* they are bereaved.

I shall commend these golden partnerships,
with children and grand-children to their name,
who never wavered from their single aim,
never forgot the vows framed by the lips
of lovers long ago, forgave the slips
from grace each other made, eschewing blame.
Such marriages have a just claim to fame,
for they are rarer than the sun's eclipse –

which one day, nonetheless, must come, as death
must come one day to close such marriages,
whose partners' dying words and final breath
express undying love and faithfulness.
Admire and emulate, applaud and bless
the ones who realise what marriage is.

A marriage is a mystery to all –
except the pair who share that secret bed
and private language, where the words unsaid
mean most, and how they speak and what they call
each other sends a message of no small
significance. They've learned the code and read
the book of marriage – know from A to Z
which silence means a welcome, which 'the wall'.

The mystery of marriage challenges
analysis: what does he see in her,
or she in him? what hidden qualities
appear – g.s.o.h. or g.i.b. –
in private? Well, perhaps the way they were
is how (together) they still seem to be.

Treasure the past, gladden today, and build
unceasingly a better future: rules
for architecture, and for marriage-schools
(if only!). Hopeful lovers might be drilled,
like architects, in principles distilled
from long experience, for only fools
refuse to learn good practice from those jewels
of wisdom, and (self-willed) remain unskilled.

Study the whole curriculum of marriage:
apology, forgiveness; say and mean,
'I love you'; practise it, and don't disparage
the *act* of love – acceptance, care and trust.
Enjoy both talk and silence, love and lust.
Nor rest until you reach the golden mean.

The art of balancing – a bike, or in
a marriage – is hard won. It can't be taught,
but must be learned through trial and error. Skin
painfully grazed, or tempers lost, have brought
the timid near to tears, but mastery
of tandem-skills is worth a few hard knocks,
harsh words, unhappy hours until the key –
once found, never again mislaid – unlocks
the mysteries of balance – on a bike,
or in a marriage. Balance is a dance
of forces, or of partners, each alike,
but different, which – performed with skill – enchants.
　The roller-coaster ride affords delight
　for those who ride together – and hold tight

120

This number, known as the 'long hundred' once,
is equal to two diamond weddings. Few
marriages manage even one! The view
of lifelong binding marriage which confronts
those newly wed, in cheerful ignorance
of what it really means, is not a true
representation of what faces you,
as you sail off in simple innocence.

Remember this: all marriages must close
in death, or disappointment, or divorce.
Death is the kindliest end that may befall
a marriage: so, when *you* both set the course
of yours, I hope you join the group that chose,
like this long sonnet-sequence, the long haul.

The rules for marriage, and for parents, and
for charities, are much the same, I guess:
expect no recompense, promote a less
dependent partnership, and understand
the hardest part – to walk away. The hand
of friendship's freely given; friends suppress
the urge to manage; then, with tenderness,
they take their leave – and ride off to their land
like Good Samaritans, whose pattern we
must follow, and whose rules we must obey:
seek neither pay nor gratitude; you'll see,
like childhood, marriage means finality –
both partners must be ready for the day
inevitable death takes one away.

Strong families and self-reliance, plus
the learning habit, make a formula
for the good life – at least, they have for us.
A marriage is a discipline, for her
and him: they both must make, and keep, the rules.
What rules? Love life, love others as you would
be loved. This is what should be taught in schools
to children – and to couples. This is good
doctrine: these rules provide a sound regime
for life and marriage. Study, read and learn;
stand on your own two feet; cherish, esteem,
love family – you'll find love in return.
   These are the regular verbs – which you must
   practise in marriage: *love* and *learn* and *trust*.

The purposes of poetry, they say –
and so do I – are threefold: to delight,
and teach, and then improve the world. That's right!
Art has a moral purpose, or it may
as well be classed as nothing more than play,
like make-up, crosswords, Scrabble ... Those who write
poems or make up stories *may* please, *might*
instruct, but *must* mend – through what they convey.

Marriage is like a poem or a tale,
which pleases, teaches, and reforms in one.
The partners should be glad to learn and grow
more patient, trustful, kinder. Never fail
to look beyond the pleasure and the fun
to find the wisdom that you need to know ...

... and practise. Knowing's useless if the truth
we know's not put to use in how we are
and what we do, in life and marriage. Youth
may *act* in ignorance, but age is far
more likely, *knowing* better, to decline
in indolence, while each forgets that we
are human *beings* first. Couples align
themselves by being kind – unceasingly.
Kindness is all: the clever, comely ones
without that quality will come to grief.
Kindness ensures that what is said and done's
harmless. Of virtues, kindness is the chief.
  Faith, hope, the other virtues, fade – you'll find
kindness, long-suffering, can still be kind.

A *marriage is a covenant: it's not
a contract*, said the preacher. Do you know
the difference? A contract's *quid pro quo* –
reciprocal allegiance – means that what
you get depends on what you give. The knot
of covenant won't slip: it means you go
on loving, come what may, in weal or woe.
(So couples who divorce have lost the plot?)

Not so. An unrepentant sinner sets
their partner free from their commitment. Where
the proffered penitence is insincere,
all bets are off. Good faith, honest regret's
essential for forgiveness. Partners must
say, and mean, *sorry* to recover trust.

Love's not a feeling, but an act of will.
In marriage, couples *choose* to love, or not.
Regardless of the wrongs – and there's a lot
that's wrong in married life – the partners still
can make a choice – to leave, or love until
life ends. A loveless marriage smells of rot –
it's not a valid choice. For love is what
we live by. Lack of love's a bitter pill
to swallow. Partners need to love and be
loved in return. On any other terms
marriage is unendurable. The pair
that shares true love affirms and reaffirms
the marriage. True love means acceptance, care
and trust, exchanged and practised ceaselessly.

We *learn to hate; and, if we learn to hate,*
we might be taught to love, Mandela claimed.
Hatred of racial difference, or a mate
(once loved), is learned – and we should be ashamed,
apologise, and seek forgiveness from
the ones we wrong. For hatred leads to wrong:
it breeds harsh words and primes the ticking bomb.
Hatred is weak and wilful – love is strong.
In marriage, the curriculum of love
is lifelong – but the pedagogy counts
for even more. *How* always ranks above
what's learned. Teach love with love in large amounts.
  It isn't what we know, or feel, but how
  we are, that makes a marriage, seals the vow.

How far shall partners go to save their mate?
Orfeo goes to hell. Fidelio,
disguised, descends to find the cell below
the gaol where Florestan bemoans his fate.
They rescue them. Some marriages await
heroic acts to save them. *Figaro*
depicts a failing marriage and the slow
decay of trust – until it seems too late ...

... to save it. But heart-felt apology,
and heart-breaking forgiveness, might revive
this moribund relationship ... who knows?
Stiffelio forgives his wife, who chose
to love another man, and keeps alive
a marriage seeming past recovery.

129

These operatic marriages depict
the quiet heroism of the home:
partners who bravely choose not to convict,
but find forgiveness for, the ones who roam
or err in other ways. *The Wife without
a Shadow*, Strauss's study of the state
of matrimony, leaves no room for doubt –
that married couples are confederate,
uniting earth and sky, the world below
the radiant splendour of the heavens above,
from which the light and dark of being flow,
in simple kindness and in selfless love.
   Sunlight and shadows, childbirth and decay –
   life ends with death, as night erases day.

Otello, Verdi's (Shakespeare's?) masterpiece
dissects a failing marriage – without trust
or closeness – showing why both partners must
communicate their fears. Domestic peace
requires care and attention: never cease
to talk and listen. What is not discussed
will fester; then, distrust becomes disgust
and hate – from which there is no quick release ...

... unless those miracles of married grace
(apology, forgiveness) save and bless
the fragile partnership. Not in this case.
Desdemona must die – her husband, too,
who learned to hate the wife he loved. Unless
you learn to love, the victims might be you!

Domestic violence is the sternest test
of marriage. How can victims love the spouse
whose words and actions violate their vows –
to love, respect and cherish for the rest
of two joined lives? Each partner who's transgressed
the laws of felony just disendows
themselves of other's trust. Nothing allows
for reinstatement till they have confessed
their crime, repented, paid the price, reformed,
and re-established trust. For violence
is no mere misdemeanour in the home;
it escalates; it kills. When wasps have swarmed,
they sting and sting without remission. Comb
the records – you'll not find a worse offence.

But what about (you ask) 'for better or
for worse'? This formula was never meant
to justify complicity in crime –
whether as partners, or aggressor and
victim. Responsibility, for sure,
lies with the guilty one: the innocent,
however, shares the blame and shame in time,
if she consents to bear the upraised hand.
Accessories include those who ignore
repeated patterns of abuse, assent
to their own harm, and sometimes even prime
the act with loose words or a rash demand.
    Duty requires the victims to depart –
    and not return without a change of heart.

A change of heart is hard to bring about –
in others or oneself – but not at all
impossible. It can't be done without
confession, penitence and training. Saul
provides a model: touched by God, made blind,
restored, baptised, renamed, he gave his life
to serve God's purpose, not his own. Unkind
spouses can learn kindness in place of strife.
It isn't easy. Attitude, routine
and practice tend in time to feel ingrained;
knowledge is useless; skills are Gadarene
herds, driven by the *spirit* that's been trained.
  A change of heart's prerequisite – and worth
  much more than all the diamonds on the earth.

For all the diamonds on the earth mean less
in marriage than the love of one good man
and wife. Their happy marriage does not bless
themselves alone, but kith and kin, and can
inspire these onlookers to emulate
the *little nameless unremembered acts*
of kindness and of love that fabricate
the best part of our lives. Marriage exacts
commitment; and, in equal measure, yields
devotion. Love engenders kindness; care
breeds care. Who learns to love in marriage wields
a magic wand, whose value is beyond compare.
  If this be error ... but it's not! It's true.
  We've proved it is – and so, we claim, may you.

I think continually of those we know,
our families and friends, who practise marriage
while moving forward through their lives. They go
on the same train, but not in the same carriage,
as we do. Every marriage is unique –
each one a journey shared by man and wife,
who choose to ride together and who seek
to shape a common purpose for their life.
Our lives are meaningless – unless we make
them meaningful. And marriage means a lot –
provided partners practise daily: take
trouble, take time, take pains, take care ... It's not
for the faint-hearted or the indolent:
hard-working spouses seem the most content.

In marriage, as in life, serenity
is found in simple, hard-won wisdom: learn
to change the things you can (yourself?), and be
content with what you can't (your partner!). Turn
away from the temptation to find fault
in others: judge yourself, if judge you must.
Advice is ill-advised, and harmful: halt,
change course, and choose acceptance, care and trust.
True wisdom lies in the distinction: what
you *can* change – what you *can't*. Your clothes, your mind,
your life – you can: the world, the weather – not.
(Nor spouse.) So, learn to be content, and kind.
  The couple who agree that nothing's wrong
  live wisely – with serenity – and long.

A marriage made on Monday's *fair of face* –
appearance is what matters, so it seems!
A marriage made on Tuesday's *full of grace* –
a marriage made in heaven ... or in dreams?
A marriage made on Wednesday's *full of woe* –
some marriages are martyrdoms, indeed.
A Thursday marriage still *has far to go* –
most marriages are marathons, agreed ...
A Friday marriage *is loving and giving* –
the *act* of love's acceptance, care and trust.
Saturday's marriage *works hard for its living* –
marriage means more than wedding cake and lust.
   The marriage made upon *the Sabbath Day*,
    I guess, will just as likely go astray!

In life, in ideology, in marriage,
we need to balance what we learn from all
the wisdom of the past – never disparage
authority – with what we may recall
from everything experienced through our lives.
Experientia docet; the past
can also teach good practice; but beware
public opinion – possibly the last
place to locate good models. We should dare
to do, think, cherish, our own way. Who thrives
by following the crowd? 'Peer-group effect'
is powerful in life, ideas – above
all else, in marriage. Wise partners select
with care their married friends – who'll teach them love ...

... for love's the answer to the questions life
and marriage, parenthood and age, propound
to child and adult, teacher, student, wife
or husband, nurse or patient. We are bound
together, bound in chains, and bound to live
by love – according to the law of love,
which teaches us we must – always – forgive,
and be as wise as serpent, soft as dove.
Love is long-suffering, and love is kind;
modest and selfless, patient, honest, calm;
resilient and strong in heart and mind.
Love takes no pleasure in another's harm.
Love means that wrongs are righted, truth prevails:
faith's fragile – hopes may fade – love never fails.

140

Who falls in love may sometimes land in marriage:
a common consequence of springtime love.
They go together — like a horse and carriage,
or Handel and Messiah, hand in glove.
Which one's the horse, or Handel, or the hand?
Which is the leader? Which one's in control?
It's true that love may lead to marriage, *and*
it's true that marriage leads to love. The soul
and heart of marriage is true love: the heart
and soul of love's the act of procreation.
The care of children is the finest part
of married life — its point and consummation.
Marriage makes sense — and families — and peace —
the world a better place — and love increase.

141

And yet, so many marriages go bad,
like rotten eggs or an infected tooth.
What hurts, and fails to work, can only add
insult to injury, like long-lost youth
consumed by gradually-advancing age.
We can't be young – but can still learn to love –
again, if we have lost the knack, or rage
replaces it, the hawk that kills the dove.
The secret is to give up being right –
yes, even when you are, and know you are!
Deprived of pride, we have no power to fight:
who lives in peace shall never bear a scar.
Humility in marriage is a must –
the seed-bed of acceptance, care and trust.

Marriage is simple, if one knows the rules:
love life, love one another, love oneself.
The Law of Love's the sharpest of the tools
available. One finds it on the shelf
marked 'Life Support': it offers kindness, care –
a kiss, a cuddle, or a cup of tea –
and confidence. It teaches one to share
life's weal and woe, its joys and misery.
Marriage is easy, if one learns to love –
a lifetime's study, and the staff of life,
the bread of heaven, rising not above
the earth, but in the hearts of man and wife.
  This is what children need to learn at school –
  then practise through their lives: the Golden Rule.

... and then it ends, when one (or other) dies.
All marriages are tragedies at last –
unless they fail before they've run their course.
Like an odd sock, or sonnet lacking rhyme,
the one who's not yet dead lives Death-in-Life –
existence without meaning, purpose, peace –
until one finds another role or use,
or death itself, the kindly one, calls time.

In time, all partnerships must fall apart.
All marriages must end, all spouses die.
And all that's left are memories of two
who practised their vocation faithfully –
reciprocal commitment, hour by hour –
for marriage is a calling, and an art.

My gross of sonnets on the great estate
of matrimony seems at last complete ...
I hope the patient reader feels replete
and satisfied – not burdened by this weight
of words, nor daunted by the solemn freight
of meaning carried on these fragile feet
in fourteen lines that constitute the neat
but narrow compass of the sonnet's 'eight-
and-six' construction – or the '3x4'
(plus 2) alternative. Should I write more?
The subject's not exhausted, but I know
I am. Read kindly what I have to show
from two long years – for better or for worse –
absorbed by marriage and engrossed in verse.